MW00744023

The Vicinity

The Vicinity David O'Meara

"But where can one find the solitude
necessary to vigour, the deep breath
in which the mind collects itself and
courage gauges its strength? There
remain big cities. Simply, certain
conditions are required."

–Albert Camus

Brick Books

National Library of Canada Cataloguing in Publication Data

O'Meara, David, 1968–
 The vicinity / David O'Meara

Poems.
ISBN 1-894078-30-6

1. City and town life—Poetry. I. Title.

PS8579.M359V52 2003   C811'.54   C2003-903572-7

We acknowledge the support of the Canada Council for the Arts,
the Government of Canada through the Book Publishing Industry
Development Program (BPIDP), and the Ontario Arts Council for
their support of our publishing program.

The painting on the cover is a detail from "No place 44" by Mara
Korkola, ©2002, oil on three 5.5" x 6" wood panels.

The author's photograph was taken by Geoffrey Brown.

This book is set in Minion and Meta.

Front cover design by Mara Korkola.

Design and layout by Alan Siu.

Printed and bound by Sunville Printco Inc.

Brick Books
431 Boler Road, Box 20081
London, Ontario   N6K 4G6

brick.books@sympatico.ca

For Dorothy Jeffreys,
my love and these words

Table of Contents

I A Civic Gesture

II Walking Around

I   A Civic Gesture

Brickwork

A red brick wall, framed
in timber beams and mortar,
collects the last gold of November warmth
on this lit morning.
It hasn't rested, though idle all these years.
A brick wall is stoic toil.
Compare one to your mother.

Or one afternoon, when an old lean-to
is removed from the back of a house,
check the darker patch left there
where sunshine did not abrade, and
consider the original
unfaded hue.

That colour is older than you.
That colour is the light from the same afternoon
as your father's father's birth.

On this corner, in this alley,
in short glimpses left
between plate glass and rolled steel, brickwork
still dogs us on our hurry to the places
we'll be meeting.
Stone-faced, it gazes on the circus
of weather. While the high-wires whistle, and gusts
trapeze between corporate blocks and a bare patch
of maples, it has composed
itself in an ordered frieze of dignity.
It wants nothing but to brace a roof
or front three-quarters of a room.
It would like to stay there—
to be a kind of proof.

Structural Steel

Make no bones
about it, the arc-welded skeleton that started
skyscrapers rolling, it's steel. Stones

once cracked from quarries, chiselled, carted,
stacked as pyramids
or devoutly spiralled into minarets, hatted

with high-pointed domes; or those svelte-gowned caryatids
carved to carry a roof-load
with support of arches, long cuts of timber, and grids

of unlikely buttresses—all told
they might cast, at most, a sixteen-storey shadow.
But then: take steel—lightweight, rolled—

and forget about base-to-height ratio:
Woolworth, Chrysler, Empire State
and Petronas—they can each thank Chicago

for starting it all. That said, of late
I've been thinking how the one thing has led
to another, the way foundations are laid—

as if I'd suddenly caught the thread
formed by the structure of I-beam and girder
and saw how steel's connected

to real estate value, higher
rents, tenements, loss of neighbourhoods, suburban
car-dependency, further

hikes in gas price, the definition
of what's West, Mid-East, Third World—the entire way
we choose to live: Clumsily. Human.

Make no bones about it, this hidden array
of iron and carbon—these stories of metal
ask us nothing but to stop someday,

look around. Raise our eyes a little.

Concrete

Inside these summer months, against
the dead-on noon, where no shadow eclipses
your grey intent focused on form alone—what you are, more

or less—wall, pillar, sidewalk, the steady civic
glue of our metropolis that faces the pedestrian
unjust jury who, in turns, condemn your ugliness

but every day embrace and raise the likes of you
from dust. What we stare into stares into us.
Each day I carry my silhouette across your sprawl;

that granular slate, un-Zen garden I plow my shadow
through, the scrawl of parking lot that's been chalked
in a hopscotch grid, children's games soon washed

away by the rain's own playfulness. You're the not-so-silver screen
our walk-on parts are posed upon; our low-budget effects,
wooden dialogue, backdrop of graffiti expletives.

Sham crust of earth, unsurprising surface, cracked
mirror to the workaday: flat, necessary, and misapplied.
Now or later, you'll show too much of us.

The Safety Elevator
(a footnote to Structural Steel)

Not
to
mention
the invention
by Elisha
G.
Otis

whose
levers
and ratchets
connected
operandi
to
modus.

Grass

Where the dew sparkles in the grass,
The spider's web waits for its prey.
The processes of nature resemble the business of men.
I stand alone with ten thousand sorrows.

              —Tu Fu

Where the dew sparkles in the grass
my Stan Smith tennis shoes have left a path
across the park. All summer long
municipal mowers buzz angrily. Grass springs
back, fills the cracks of everything.

The spider's web waits for its prey
while the spider's off-stage, between benchslats,
unhurried and deliberate like the Chinese
grandmothers I watch practicing Tai Chi. Does this
gesture mean "waving hands in clouds" or "go away please?"

The processes of nature resemble the business of men.
How to compare? Fried eggs, filtered coffee, then
watch everyone go into the dog-eat-dog.
It will rain this afternoon; I know from the radio.
Good for the grass. How to compare?
Business is good in southern Ontario.

I stand alone with ten thousand sorrows.
Work, eat, sleep. Bills, laundry, traffic. Poor
me. What else—? Worse, Tu Fu, than loneliness?
The earth I touch I never reached for.
I have no right to speak of grass.

Glass

Whatever it is you see, you see. But see,
it's not like that. *That* is what's beyond here, and here
is this. And whatever lies between is glass.

All you can see is what's perfectly clear, though clear
to say it's never quite there, like air or innuendo. Like
speaking in the past tense. Ask

the bird that saw its graceful arc
cleaving a path from that to this, and instead, kissed
glass. Ask yourself, in several shirts, buttoned

up guiltily over each other, what were the properties
of that two-way mirror? In short, you're both going nowhere
fast. Forget it. That is our habit with glass.

Wire

A phone rings, a light comes on, but not here.
How long have I slouched in the candled dark, drinking beer

(gone warm) with my shadowy double inside the wall's projected halo?
The storm wind resounds, a cathedral's effect of deep tremolo

that shakes thin glass in its frames. What's a dog think when it howls?
                                                    Someone
will hear, someone will hear. That stubborn cry is a prayer he'll hone

on the wind's sharp rasp all night. The lines are down. No sudden
                                        power will light
the dim conception in his eyes, no voice say "C'mon boy, it's all right,

don't be afraid." Quieter now, he haunts the steel-mesh cage
in my landlady's yard, scratches and paces in the outage.

Too civilized to yelp or whine, I guard the candle's meagre fire.
I sit and wait. I pray to wire.

Rooftop

                                    Poof,
we're there, had dragged ourselves up, out
from the womb of streetlamp
                circles and one-room apartments,
and pushed on into that other level,

the ur-floor of antennae, air-vents, skylight tents
of wire-lined glass pitched
                on tar and crushed gravel.

Nothing stirred but tree-crowns and hedges down below
that swelled and collapsed like lungs,
as we squatted by the verge, small as buttons sewn
beneath the sidereal ruff of the Milky Way.
Our coats hung
stiff as the first flags on the moon.

Cheers. (The clink of bottles).
Now what? Sit? Listen
to the tinny rattle of street-level
conversation, laughter, a carhorn's ululation…
or skulk like prison-campers along the cornice,
leer through angled shutters
for swivels of flesh,
roll pebbles down the gutter-pipes,
spook the tabbies, or chug
and scatter when the cop-cars show,

hangdog and unconvincingly surprised
in their flashlight's flare
when they call,
                        "Boys,
you'd better get down from there"
before they confiscate our alcohol.

No, it wasn't like that
at all.
Our other life goes largely unrecorded.
We existed in the heaving air for fifteen minutes
like any squirrel or bird that's settled
on this secret world, one foot

         out and one foot
in it.
Not much happened
but the rustling that's inside us.
We left three empties
with a finger of beer—
perhaps still there—as proof we came, like
burned-down candles in a forest cabin.

In the future, everyone should be unheard of
for a quarter of an hour.

The Basilica at Assisi

Lift. Lift. Point my chin
and follow it up to the hillside.
Sweat strolls down the bridge to my nose-tip,
swells,
drops—I smear
my palms with dirt
to cake a handhold. Then it's
bend the back, compress
the spine, lift, swing torso, grit
teeth, breathe, breathe, push
and fight this load past every cypress
and speck of dusty road.

If I could swear and still be pious.

Oh, I took this grunt work
for room and board and a few
measly lira—the best you can
hope for in 1233 A.D.—if
you're not a bishop already, just
a knuckle-dragger like myself in a town
like Assisi. Word is, if
you're wondering, this basilica's
in honour of some local hero
best remembered
for stripping down to nothing and talking to the birds.
In short, what
anyone could manage with a few
jugs of vino and some birdlime.
Those still around who'd seen him
in his heyday claim he was an eyeful:
living off stale heels of bread and tree sap,
working the odd miracle, barefoot
as a baby, mangy
and about as dazed
as a she-wolf in a bear pit.
But boy, could he talk—! Talk a storm

into a rain barrel, convince a plum
into a pie crust.
And it's said that on his deathbed
he sat his sorry body up
and begged it to forgive him
for all he'd made it suffer…
                              Get that.
Try humping granite
from a quarry till dusk
on a lunch of boiled turnips and weasel-piss,

or what I'm getting good at: hauling
wet plaster in a wheelbarrow
that's slapped and smoothed across walls
in a mess
              they're calling fresco.

Then it's brick and mortar, brick
and mortar, to complete the clerestory
by our deadline—*This time*
next century is the joke
going round, if the heat and food don't finish us first.
It could be worse I guess,
denounced for heresy and tied up to the stake
like that Fraticelli sect who kept
making noises about their cult
of poverty, bare in the face
of the selfsame Pope who's funding this little project.
As for me, once we're done, I figure
with a couple references
there's a better than even chance
I can get out of this burg

to Urbino or maybe Florence
where the real money is—

The Valley Temples of Egypt

Let's not think how nothing lasts.
It is always noon and always dusk there;
a dry reed-yellow light is slanting off

through naves and hollow sanctums, strewn
with broken shafts and column parts
like scattered stubs in an ashtray.

The mind sparrows out over mud flats
and narrow floodplain. Over delta, porticos,
a laid-out causeway, aisles of ram-headed statues,

dead kings who each contain the ponderable
trinity of stone, sand and dust, that quietly race toward
the null precipice where every progress ends.

It is always noon and always dusk where
nothing lasts. It is always soon, and never.
Whenever I try to think of a place

that old, I need a drink, or some closed
room of perfect blackness, or
a windy canyon to spit down into.

I need the steep obliterating fall
of something deep and blank; that pharaonic
stillness of four thousand years

less of history hoping to know
what eternity is, and come so close
it seems further away, like squinting to glimpse

the eyelash on your own eyeball.

The Unhappy Condition

*"Such was the unhappy condition of the Roman emperors, that
whatever might be their conduct, their fate was commonly the same."*

— Edward Gibbon

On that subject, let me
comment: that the wide
populace had endured twelve years
of forced flattery, general terror, and private groans
is well-known; witness to state and senate
dissolving from idle suspicions into public blood—
The miscreant whimsy of Commodus still
bruises civic memory.
Twelve years multiplied by his lusts and purges.
A terrible equation
only his servants solved: Maria,
the favoured concubine, laced his drink, and while
he slept, a local wrestler held his throat
perfectly shut.

And such was the mistrust heightened by those years
that when, in the same late hour, ancient Pertinax
rolled half-aware
to find the wild-eyed crew
of domestics circling his bed, he uncurled
and lay prone, prepared for death. Instead

they offered the throne of the Roman world.

Some eighty-six days was the proof of their enlightened assessment.
Hasty in virtue, Pertinax cut
Imperial comforts, replaced pilfered fortunes, called exiles home.
History will record the esteem of his people.

I am also witness to that fact, and to the Praetorian Guards' jealousy.
For one good reason or another, it fell to me
to level the first sufficient blow
and the rest of them tore him to pieces.

Nomad

Gafsa to Tozeur, three abreast, in
the back, piled close on wheezing station-
wagon seat-springs, the hood-stripe
cutting yawned-at early light
through olive groves and rollers of desert sand.
One hour, tops. South-west,
south-west. I could feel his hand
nudge near my ribs as it grappled
inside the brown-wool scarps of his cloak.
For what? I tried to guess.
A tool. Bread? It might have been, for all I know,
a cellphone. His face was an auburn stone,
submitting no evidence of the prolonged
spelunking at his torso
as he wrangled with the driver over every dinar,
a taut fringe of frayed white cloth
pegged behind his ears, the soft linen
polishing a bald scalp that crowned the furrowed
carapace of his brow and forehead, dry
as the salt-cracked sufferance of the Chott-el-Jerid.

Then a wide shapeless sleeve
puffed and filled, slunk
lengthwise to the cuff, like the digestive
bulge of a snake's latest meal, and the nomad's
fist appeared, clutching rumpled currency. And
that hand, his right:
like leather. Like dark sandpaper.
                              I know
I stared when he opened his palm, finely white,
buffed and smooth. Half of three fingers and the top
of his thumb were gone, forgotten
since the mishap that fused the stump of index
to middle. The hand withdrew, deep inside, then his face
beneath the hood. The rough scratch of road
stretched on, under the magnifying sun.

Houses in Small Towns

These are the great homes of pine and brick
anchored to crests along wide river-valleys.
Once raised by textile and lumber barons,
another century's still-tangible clouds
darken their windowpanes.

They do not fit with the picture you've been handed;
not in crew-cut, whitewashed innocence
or that desperate, fucked-up meanness
portrayed in a novel's darkest fictions.
The truth is

they're suspended somewhere between abuses
of alcohol, children, and other extremes hardly
guessed at—search those second-floor drapes when going
past, you'll as likely see someone dying slowly
from boredom.

But those porches and backyards may still remain
the neutral space where we all begin, ushered
from dreams through knowing looks and bitter years
into a gentle equilibrium. But why is the reaching so
hard there?

We know a little of these things—portraits that stare
through a white banister at doors and upstairs halls,
the twice-tapped departure of a car-horn,
the empty street, the smell of raked-up grass mounds
across level lawns.

Photograph of the Funeral Pyre of Pol Pot

"Keeping you is no gain. Losing you is no loss."
— an aphorism of the Khmer Rouge

I look at the picture again. A mattress, padding
stitched to rolled edges, flat above the dusty
raft of black tires,
laid out in the choked brush of a clearing: last materials
purged from the junk-pile site of everyday things,
that warehouse of essential and useless effects.
And desk, rags, a blanket, legs-up rattan chair, another tire mixed
with wispy twigs

—they start to flare, crackle, kick up into the delicate slashes
of orange and red, that shouldn't,
from the look of it,
possibly raise real heat or spread—
Doubtful this stack
will ever lick off flesh, organs, all
the rind that's wrapped
on bone, to finally disperse the despotic whiff of the self.

But now
one soldier has brought the first real wood to the scene:
a solid heft of dry, twisted
tree-trunk. He eyes the heap
of furniture and tangled bric-a-brac.
Should he heave the log on top, or leave it angled against the side?
It won't catch, he's thinking. The thin branches
will collapse and just blow off, the mattress
is probably damp, and those tires, if they light, just
churn up inky smoke and stink.

And this figure on the right, another soldier, looks away, very still,
as if guarding a small drop of sweat rivering to his tailbone,
or focused on a bird's shrill cackle.
Is this history? The hesitant display of things we can't touch,

a place

where people enter and never come out?
I look at the picture. It could be anywhere:
this backdrop of leaf-cover,
the straight trees, the jig-sawed swatch of sky just
over there.

To the Minotaur

*"…the Minotaur is boredom. For some time the citizens…have given
up wandering. They have accepted being eaten."*

—Albert Camus

I sometimes think of you, shambling
across the factory floor you never saw the last of,
conveyor-belt assembly line in July's
slow choke-hold: shiftwork
of taking apart and putting what's left

back together, killing the hours one blah tick
at a time. I can still read the numbers
on that punch-card, still see your diehard
stubborn face, nose-ring, and home-carved tattoo:
a ship with black sails anchored in your tricep.

The troubled youth in movies we were dragged to
had nothing on us. We never saw the credits
of *Risky Business*: you drank a gin mickey,
on acid, and passed out in the toilet stall. We never
thought someone might pop up in the obits. That,

or tear the town apart, chew up the other reckless few
who got too close. I remember fists
through windows, arrests at school dances, or taking
chances in the family Olds, blowing doughnuts
through the snow in warehouse parking lots,

those games of how we'd get where we were getting
without touching the brake, a no-winner dare
that often bluntly ended in the unsnapped tension
of guardrail wires, or brunt of county ditches.
Out of your head, you must have thought

you were immortal. Well, maybe we all did.
Same crowd, different bodies passed around
in a puerile juggle of booze, lust, and vague vocation
we never cleanly kept aloft—instead, just honed
the art of hanging out, cinched and spun
in the town's rough limits,

islanded, incestuous, messed-up as our parents,
too dumb to wish for fate's more graceful options.
Last time I was back this way, I passed the dives
we squabbled in, had words, traded blows. I took it
on the chin, followed my own thread, and lit out

for good. Memory might be another name for all
those fabulous screw-ups in the past, stunts
and escapades of suspect myth, but the wasted
unheroic hours must be reckoned with. They are where
we live: rooms and years where nothing happens.

Day Planner

Keep it:

the Morse-prodding beep
of alarm—get set, go—bottle-neck creep
in the newest car, the elevator
ride to a higher floor.
Phone calls, staff meeting, fax;
early lunch, make tracks.

Save it:

microwave and drive-through,
heavy on the pedal—*move! will you*—
Car horn, shortcuts, double park;
the early worm gets to work.
Hard sell. Can't talk, no to or fro.
Things to do, people to see, places to go.

Kill it:

smoke break. After five, some beers—
talk shop, grind the gears.
Knock that ball around the course,
movie rental, sex with spouse.
Say goodnight to the enemy, the children;
cut the light, pray to heaven.

At the Aching-Heart Diner

She will flavour her coffee with both cream and sugar
and tap on the window as she mentions the weather,
tossing off sparks when she pulls off her sweater.
The waiter will come. She'll give her order
bluntly: "A hot chicken sandwich and a tall glass of water."
She'll spatter her french fries in grand doses of vinegar
and the point she is making, emphasize with a gesture,
her steak knife held high like a gravy-stained scimitar.
And the salt that is scattered when she topples the shaker
she'll toss with a flourish across her left shoulder.
I'd like, I will say, to get to know you better.
I'll look down at my clubhouse, so we don't look at each other
as I pull out the toothpick that holds it together.

Fountain

Not the intricate engineering wrought
by the hands of antiquity; not
the modern touch of electric pumps and tubes.
Not the micturition of famous cherubs,

or efflux from a fish's Gillespie spout.
Not the lilies cloying there. Don't think about
them, or the rusting pennies that tourists
threw, or the ones clutched now, tightly, in their fists.

Not the marble General in his stirrups,
or the midnight reflection of the moon.

Just this pool that's stirred by the double spoon
of brassy, half-dressed lovers, in their cups.

Riding the Escalators

Let's get lost in everything
as we glance around. The escalator cycles
from the clearance shelves in the bustling concourse,
and up into 2nd, 3rd, 4th floors.

As we glance around, the escalator cycles.
It's an unbroken arrangement of progress.
And up into 5th, 6th, 7th floors
we're shuttled through clothes, sportsgear, perfume, appliances.

It's an unbroken arrangement of progress,
the fashion and accessories
we're shuttled through: clothes, sportsgear, perfume, appliances.
We are looking for something to catch our eye.

The fashion and accessories
reverse in sequence on the mirrored descent.
We are looking for something to catch our eye.
The warm rubber handrails, the escalator steps

reverse in sequence on the mirrored descent.
Knick-knacks, time-savers, coffee-table books,
the warm rubber handrails, the escalator steps…
Descending, we might price each item in order.

Knick-knacks, time-savers, coffee-table books,
children's toys, luggage, souvenirs…
Descending, we might price each item, in order
to imagine what a bit more cash could buy—

children's toys, luggage, souvenirs—
from the clearance shelves in the bustling concourse.
(Imagine what a bit more cash could buy…)
Let's get lost in everything.

Poem for King Kong

Smoggy day. The sky's soft palm. Skyscraper
in it, so high, it unrolls a shadow blocks-long
and broken over rooftops. Gulls snicker up there;
say har-dee-har, haw haw haw.

Poor voyeur like us—nervous, a little turned on.
Is it the corner ledge's view, so tall and far,
and far, that knocks the breath right out of you?
A drop like that won't fit the body well.

Open wide, say *ah*. It's going to hurt a bit,
this fog of love, homelessness, a hundred floors of metal,
glass and carpet you're dropping past. Oh peripheral
nudged-aside being, count them as you fall.

Poise

— for Andrea Skillen (1968-2002)

I see that steady beauty mark
and hear your clear dissenting voice say
oh c'mon, as I scratch this note to you
on a low, wet day in summer.

You wouldn't want the fuss, I know, nor
trust the souped-up sentiment—it's just
I'm trying to arrange a parting batch
of verse before we all get too disorganized, stray

far apart, forget the dates of birthdays
you'd have marked inside your calendar. (Strange
to think that in a certain numbered space
you've stopped, and we keep going on.)

If it scares me in the future that
things we did might blur, get lost, as if you'd
slipped off to a back room in a badly-lighted
bar with greying carpets, I equally know

your footwork on the dance floor
or that purple grin of lipstick will not
escape remembering. Just as we won't soon
forget that hospital bed, the undying

laughter there, and you and Claire grown
more beautiful with courage.
The word I'm thinking of is *poise*, why
we'll miss you greatly in the years

that come, and wonder what you'd say, each
semblance of your remembered wit reminding us how
whole years pass by without telling
our friends how much we love them,

so I'm telling them now.

From a Dawn Taxi

"Me, I start at 4:00," the cabbie says, then wrestles
the gearshift till it grinds, finds its slot, hunkers
down into first.
His short-wave throws static,
crackling out of Europe. It's a whole
other day there and he's already in it, while
I'm in the back, with night's final fringes.

I like the slippery minutes of a dark and tiny hour.
Only a few conspire with this cobalt-
blue air. The streetlamps bead past my window
like a string
of lambent pearls, the darker gaps between them
whipping softly across our faces. Like frames
you never see on a turning reel of film.

The cabbie checks his clock, trades a thick accent
with the hoarse voice at dispatch, then troubles
the dial on his radio.
Failed peace-talks, late-breaking reports
from the world… The car slips through amber, its tail-lights
leaving the tinted street behind—the storefronts and corners,
a bridge's arc. Another morning in history.

The Turofsky Collection

—for Don Coles

In one of Lou and Nat Turofsky's famous photos,
it's a tight scrum in front
of the Red Wings' crease,
Sawchuk on his pads, leaning forward, keen
but anxious for the imminent
outcome of jabs,
shoves, slashes. The two teams manhandle
the busy space
between them, digging
through shins for possession. The Leafs,
one goal down—it's late
in the third—
have pulled their goalie, so now it's a rare chance
to eyeball the twelve players
all together, grappling
inside the black and white frame of late 50s Toronto,
while familiar names—
Pulford, Howe, Mahovlich, Horton—
fasten to each other, fully and presently tensed
for the possible puck to snap out
from those mangled
inches of action. The referee, in zebra jersey, splayed legs
kinked at the knees,
lips his whistle
at the edge of whatever could've been, blunt potentials
still pure from their not-yet
having occurred.

Lou must have snapped this one, his dear brother dead, oh
going on three years now.
Hard, after all that,
to arrive alone. Once the game's decided, he'll take it
on the heel-and-toe, down
to the studio
on Queen Street, like they'd always done, have the prints
ready for next
morning's paper.

This time next year he'll be gone, collapsed
near the blue-line boards, this picture
            the last of his
pre-playoff seasons, nights puffing Punch Lily cigars,
press camera in hand at the Gardens.

            Most important here
are the men's dark suits, the fancy hats of the women.
They are taking their places
            in the stacked history
of sport, graciously believing the determined tide
must change to favour them
            while they linger there,
as if dressed for dinner, breath held and attendant
on the hoped snapshot
            we all would sit for,
the sweeter memories amid so much loss. Scattered pin-points
of reflected light
            flash from their horn-
rimmed glasses, signalling to us from the hard benches
of the arena's receding decades.
            Distant stars,
they hold the past and are probably gone. While back there,
in the half-lit corridor
            of a minute's fraction
that occupies space just beyond this photograph, Red Kelly
will be the lucky one,
            first to control
that loose puck off the scramble—geez, he'll think, *geez*—
and sail its curt lump
            into the open
abandoned net. Obvious we possess that truth at least. Detroit 4,
            Toronto 2.

From a Stopped Train

—for Ken Babstock

Now that I have some time alone—a stolen
hush in the bustle of our social selves—
I'd like to give some warm applause
to oxygen, to water, to all those usual taken-
for-granteds. Like silence. Or the little space
inside my head which says it doesn't matter what time
the train gets in, that's just now paused its
stretched-out pulse on this track somewhere

near Brockville, near Smiths Falls.
Then behind the fold-out tray that dis-
articulates from a gadget inside my armrest, I am staring
into the drift of Ontario midnight, that's bereft
of all but the smallest twinkles of farm or star,
so the glass becomes a mirror, or a specimen slide
of dark fields and stillness and moonlight
where I'm pinned like a struggling insect,

dissected, nudged nearer to some old failure
I might stew inside, left to taste that tart hard centre
in the sugary self, or hear a music of pained discovery.
Then the train-length judders into motion,
a stylus on night's black vinyl—
In an hour, there's me with the platform breeze, mass
transit, shouts and horns, the talk and drink
in crowded bars. I should be grateful for the noise.

Abandoned Movie-House

No bulbs left, just a blackened
row of sockets and sprigs of slashed wire.
Nudged around by spring drizzle,
soiled pigeons lurk in the marquee's bare frame,
cooing and dripping grey excrement like candle wax.
Posters for ska and punk bands overlap on exits
boarded-up with plywood, where weeks

are counted off with cracks from a staple gun.

They must echo inside; faint depth-charges thumping
above the unrecoverable past.
Below chipped rococo swirls on the painted ceiling,
five hundred seats face the blank
suggestion of spectacle
paused between reels for all
the so-called ever. Outside, high

on its crumbling facade—once an office
or projection room—there's
the rubbed rheumy eye of a window, still intact,
that blinks when a cloud blots the sun.
I might have fine-tuned my aim and slung
a few rocks up there
just a few years back, if only to burn off

some mean undirected compulsion. But now,
when my route bends me past, I check
on that glass, wish it well,
quietly guarding its fragile endurance.
Maybe I'm going soft. It must be
what they mean about getting older.

To a Friend

You're halfway there now.
I can see you, car wheels spitting
arcs of water off the rain-glossed highway,
a bleached slate of Monday sky
hung dully above Alberta.

After such time away, that sweet
retreat into a different space, your thoughts
must turn toward routine
and all the little dramas outside the self
that spark and slowly burn toward you

on the wick of each kilometre.
You must be tired. Hand on the wheel, you must
be crow-eyed between the gusts of two
quite different lives. At gate
twenty-three, I wish you good weather,

and watch them load my plane, imagine
its slick wings and hundred-tonne
fuselage sliding through clouds anyone
should be speechless to dwell in,
contours and dark shadows skittering past below.

One day a phrase might come to describe
this all. Maybe it will enter me
at 37,000 feet, as my flight begins
its controlled descent to a world
we didn't seem attached to.

Or it may find you as you stop,
stretch, fill the tank, gaze
toward the hours left to go, the long
sharp ridges and continuous hills,
the criss-crossing streets of home.

Sister

I'm still here, sister.
You're there. I forgot.
You were the subject
we dropped all winter.

Talk is you're back,
you've been seen around.
They say the rate you're
going, you're bound

to burn up, burn out.
They want me to care.
That dark day, I'm
glad I won't be there

to see it happen,
or the terrible mess
you'll leave with your wake.
My selfishness then,

the trouble I'm turning
a blinded eye to. Still
sister, burn.
I will always look up to you.

Letter to Auden

Well then, sir, I thought of you again just recently:
    New Year's ticked in with scant fuss,
  The so-called millennium, hyped
    To bring disaster—not quite the end of us
But certainly an indisputable wholesale mess.
    There *was* noise, drunkenness,
    Fist-fights, cab-shortages, looters—
  But nothing resembling accidents
    Caused by crashed computers.

Nothing collided at midnight but our glasses in hand, then
    We hugged, blew horns, and kissed,
  While everyone across the globe,
    If not in bed, were pissed
On vodka, lager, chardonnay, so for one night at least
    Most aggression had ceased
    And the future seemed certain and stable
  (Though a good friend of mine raced round the room
    And flattened the coffee table).

I'm sure you'd like some gossip, who's out and what's come in,
    The inside scoop on movers
  And shakers, the current poetic forms,
    (If anyone writes light verse
Anymore, if some of your books are still selling…)
    That job might be overwhelming
    But the world's much the same: factions at odds
  Over money or race, and—as always—
    Incompatible gods.

Yes, you'd find our mixed-up planet feels far too familiar—
    We can hardly cry a
  Tear as we wipe each other out;
    So long as some Messiah
Can be called upon, we march united to one grandiose Nada,
    The unlimited Florida
    Of history's retirement. Religion
  Will marinate us the way *we* sauced
    The passenger pigeon

As we shell out millions on Roman candles that take one
    Quarter-hour to exhibit
  While the gene pool shrinks, the ice-caps melt,
    And forests go to shit.
We must look real fine to those Emperors of history
    Who didn't mind infamy
    If it showed a little panache.
  Sir, I like what you said: *This great*
    Society is going smash.

It's not really that we've ceased to care; we *never* did.
    But back when we were wrapped
  In skins, didn't have a match to burn,
    Ate with our fingers, and crapped
In the woods without benefit of Handi-wipe,
    We could bear to have the type
    Who fly right off the handle, crack,
  And commence a reign of Holy
    Terror, but at worst attack

A few weak cousins in our tribe and steal our fire.
    Oh, we like to notice how
  Barbaric our kind could be back then,
    How fine we're sitting now,
And shake our heads at Genghis Khan, the Viking raids,
    Inquisitions, and long Crusades;
    But those secure in that quaint notion
  The worst offences are in old texts,
    Disregard commotion

Reported in the T.V. news and daily papers
    And pine to think that Goebbels
  Was sent here from some other planet
    With Gulf Wars and Chernobyls.
And sir, I understand, if the bio I read was yours,
    You were around for two World Wars
    And witnessed the dread atrocities
  Of Spain's troubled clash—not to mention
    The Sino-Japanese—

So it's grim to quote you the latest stats, which school-kids
    Haven't had to study yet,
  But the recent span that joins these centuries
    Could just be the bloodiest.
Our weapons, quite new, are still as highly distressful
    Though now they're more successful
    And are televised when they kill.
  Nothing's changed. We have our madness
    And our weather still.

But the recent trend that might disturb you, more than
    Committees awarding
  Olympic-medal status to Beach
    Volleyball and Snowboarding,
Is the growing flair we have for being targeted
    With stylish, well-marketed
    Must-have technological gadgets—
  (Apologies to Guinness on their
    ingenious floating widgets…)

Fax, e-mail, cellphones, the Net: you should see the stuff
    We've thunk up since you died.
  Fast-food restaurant drive-throughs
    And electric toothbrushes aside,
There is no finer delusion that we're saving time
    Than this busy pantomime
    Of screens, links, beeps and double-clicks
  As if we'll turn our twenty-four hours
    One day to twenty-six.

Now we never waste an hour on antique hobbies
    Like sitting in silence
  Or whittling wood. What's the use of
    All that awful patience
When a thousand stimuli are ours to sample
    On-line? For example:
    No one needs to bother writing verse or
  Stories anymore; one button's
    Touch will make a cursor

Wink out crack programs like makegoodpoetry dot com.
　　Just key in your preference
　For mood, style, or form; pick a tone,
　　(Moral outrage, for instance),
Suggest some treasured images from heartfelt theme-words—
　　Flowers maybe, or birds,
　　A season, or place-names near your home
　To give it local colour. Press
　　Enter: You've got a poem.

Without our pesky human meddling, paperbacks will
　　Soothe like Vick's Vapo-rub,
　And doubtless find their way inside
　　An Oprah-type of Book Club.
Our legacy in this Newest Age, like railroads
　　In the last, are bar-codes,
　　Micro-chips and encoded files
　That make generic products fit
　　Around our tele-lifestyles.

High-tech firms and franchise now shape the Things-to-Be—
　　Really, why begrudge them?
　　(Anyone in opposition
　　Is clearly a curmudgeon
And thinks it quaint there's home-cooked meals, virgin woodland,
　　And letters written longhand.)
　　Euro-banknotes and Bill Gates
　Have duly compressed the world's breadth
　　More than tectonic plates

So that pretty soon we'll share the same opinions,
　　Swallow the same cuisine,
　　Dress in fashions dictated by
　　One glossy magazine
And pause with ironic smirks for history to pop
　　Its last champagne and stop
　　Unfolding altogether. Then
　We won't have to bustle about
　　Trying to make things happen

Since there's plenty of old stuff just lying around.
  We've got Greek pottery,
 Roman aqueducts and temples,
 Pisa's tower (though tottery),
That Big Wall in China; Mozart opera; Be-bop, Blues;
  English sonnets, Haikus;
 Moroccan rugs and German beer,
 Cuban cigars—Ok, I'm skipping
 Over quite a lot here—

But history, more than ever, is now a snazzy show
  Put on for the tourists,
 As if no one lives here anymore
 And culture just exists
To sell, promote, consume, and generally entice
  Travellers to our merchandise.
 (And correct me here if there's some doubt,
 But wasn't the Great Wall constructed
 To keep the tourists *out*?)

Sir, enough; I must admit, since looking back over
  The past eighteen stanzas
 It seems *I've* wandered from the point.
 (There is no rhyme but Kansas.)
In this lyric's first line I had started to say
  How the last New Year's Day
 You'd been on my mind. Why? Who knows.
 It's true I'd completed, in just
 Seven months, not one but two bios

That described your duration. And lately, I'll add
  I have mostly inspected
 The crowded near-thousand pages
 That forms your *Collected*.
You've memorable lines, are unrivalled with meter
  —You knew where your feet were
 And quite happy to show it—
 In the end, sir, I'll attest, you're
 One impressive poet.

Maybe the danger of our frequent disregard
    Was what you might have meant
    About our damaged lot as humans,
    Which sent me on my tangent
Of bellyaching about the post-post-modern condition.
    If our one ambition
    Could be to close the gap between
    Our public and private faces
    Then happiness might mean

Attending, at last, to what is most commonplace:
    Unbounced cheques, our neighbours'
    Warm affection, the friendship of rooms
    With sun and hardwood floors,
(If only life could arrange itself neatly as a rhyme,
    Or the balanced way we climb
    And relax inside a hammock)
    But nothing we'll ever know is that
    Patly epigrammatic—

As if our existence were one simple rule that campers
    Practice when residents
    Of the woods: *Take nothing but photos;*
    Leave nothing but footprints.
Who can say with assurance that the wide scowl of Age
    Will temper its umbrage,
    Unwrinkle, and offer a cheek;
    That the verse you gave form to
    Will be noticed next week

Or judged far too stiff and irrelevant, and you
    An outdated denizen
    From some other century, the way
    We think now of Tennyson.
Maybe the dates we live inside are unfixed borders
    Which we get our orders
    To move across one day, no word
    That our part was even successful,
    That our values endured,

But these first days of the newest year, of taking
  Stock and inspecting the view,
I caught myself looking backward,
  And Wystan, I spotted you.
With ashtray, drink and carpet slippers, you still seemed bent
  In keen astonishment
  On naming the plague of our neuroses,
  Suggesting those who suffer worst
  Prescribe the better doses.

Truth is, I've no good reason for writing you this letter;
  It's rife with mixed regards—
The way we feel true warmth for friends
  While cheating them at cards.
Perhaps I need forced rhyme, or idle chit-chat *entre nous*
  To guess what Dante knew
  Justifies champagne: something about love,
  Interest, praise, and gratitude,
  Or all of the above.

II Walking Around

"Cities also believe they are the work of the mind
or of chance, but neither the one nor the other
suffices to hold up their walls. You take delight
not in a city's seven or seventy wonders, but in
the answer it gives to a question of yours."

–Italo Calvino

Solvitur ambulando–"it is solved by walking"

Rough Directions

The exact way back is fading, indistinct
like the shine after brief rain, when a soft
ether-veil of haze hangs in open vistas between apartment
blocks, like the abandoned quiet of cul-de-sacs, or escapes
into bars on a tossed-away lazy Saturday.
Along that street—I can't remember the name—of storefront glass
kid-scribbled in traceries of January's taut frost,
by those homeless human shapes bent
in the steam of a laundromat vent.
Down the boulevard: a balcony in oak shade, just
one flight up, that noses its ledge toward the park's
soccer field; past an Art Deco facade, where ornate iron banisters
curl to the one-room spread
of hardwood floor, tulip-glass lampshades,
a Murphy bed, and radiators that knock
far more than visitors.

On the corner, down further, there's
a coffee place, open twenty-four hours, penned with a plot
of narcosis and long espressos, page-
turning as the roll of its cigarette smoke,
where someone sits, waiting. Turn right, I guess,
past Doric-flanked bank lobbies, by half-thought-of shops;
near afternoons, and summer, where shadows lengthen and lean
into all-of-the-sudden dust-devils that are born
and expire in ten-second lives
across the edges of parking lots. Past the pong of fish markets, head shops,
and delicatessens, where waiters
in rolled-up sleeves have locked up for the night, had one quick drink,
                                                                and stroll
to barely-known neighbourhoods.
Along other streets, certain corners, whole
evenings not found on any map. Memory,
you can go there. Down Some-such Avenue,
Rue Saint Whatever.

The Weather

I

Warm, then cold. Then
           warm again.
Bright days.
Rain. For weeks,

the melt and runoff—
then interrogation by sun, that
sadistic senorita with a rose
in her teeth, grinning. Then

rain. And bright days.

II

Then wind at the street corner, wind
at the doorframe—no, please,
after *you*—wind, as civil servant, pushing papers
along curb lengths, against a baseball
diamond's backstop, filed under autumn.

Rain-clouds in wet swabs. Edged
soak of darkness coming down.

The canal's mirror-surface
shattering endlessly, its sound
a standing ovation…

III

As I walk, all of me
      is on the skin, is in
the eyes, clipping, then releasing the small
hasps of attention.
I'll get out from where the crowds go,
the bars about to close,
              to where
streetlights picket the city limits

and a cold front
ruffles the worn hem
                    of clover fields
far out there under stiff tarps of blackness.
Wide stiff winter days.
The lightest frost-veil tightens the current.

Slush-dirty streets
criss-cross through the white
blocks of houses in snow, weaving
a December tartan.

     IV

No need to look long out windows—
                    when we were young and half-listening
wisdom got away from us. With that head start,
we won't catch
up before the end.
So the weather takes us
                    like a tipsy usher
to wait in the dark-varnished pews
that we call our years.

What are we?

Sheet lightning cupped in a valley.

     V

The weather whispers, "pack just
one bag, leave the rest behind"

and everything you ever spent money
to own says
"you're no cowboy."

VI

Spring now. Warm, cold, then
warm again.
Puddles in the schoolyard.

(That first day out,
                    coatless…)

Thin
splinters of ice huddle in the shadows
of buildings, dissolve into the grass.
Drippings needle through coniferous and concrete

down where the canal and river met,
together now
for so long they seem inseparable,
                                glad
but hesitant,

as if they had married too young.

Thinking and Feeling

Storm-clouds roam dusk.
Smaller bodies scram hole-ward. Bristle
of treetops,
overlapped flashes…
                        Patience
ties another slip-knot to ruin
                and holds 'er steady.

Walking around today, a cameo in wind's
little dramas,
nothing to do but be somewhere, maybe finish
an abandoned crossword while
the window-frame broadcasts a downpour.

Prime conditions to brood.
The brain
picks its own lock, selects from each
tightly-rolled worry, those
ochre stogies in the skull's bone humidor,

lights one,
chomps and puffs.
                Better,

that. Better to method-act this unease
than be typecast as clumsy
                        in the feel-good scenes.
Best to be here insistently, even if
half-shaped and grey
in day's ultrasound.
Still looming down,
                        embroidery
of human things
and weather…

Though we've put our hours in, no
paycheque is waiting for how we think and feel—mixing
our palette of blue tones
for the still-
life of evening,

or posed, hands folded, eyes gazing into
the common of this
                    idle everything.

If our life could tell us, if we could
thresh what's so serious
flat. Like mint
or dandelion, the more we try to diminish
doubt, words put
root, whole phrases raise new second thoughts
                              from the brow's
absorbed furrows.
They ache and grow as grief, atonement, anger,

lost love and kept love,
visible in the cracks of any fulfillment.

Window, an etch-a-sketch
of rain, scratches these questions, a chain-
letter mailed, mailed, mailed
to myself again.

What goes on in the mind, each memory, scene
I look into—old, low home of living
torn down
and rebuilt by any simple qualm. Stupid

to not
remember you.

Fun

Glad interim, your line-ups
stretch past sidewalk patios,

those polyester pastels and unbuttoned plunges
of neckline deepen

this brio of cologne, neon, and patter.
Nice shoes. Great hair.

Walk me past here, in the swing of this compunction.
The street, summer-stung, swells,
                                    infected.
You're a grin in the gut, buzz
in the breastbone, a straightaway where
                        energy can rev heavy on the throttle, then just open
up.

In a cave of strobe and blacklight,
some rock outfit, guitars slung low, clutch garage-
chord euphoria. Bass drum,
snare,
scintillant snap and shrug of cymbal-pools
                        shuck through waves of sound.
Everyone moves, keelhauling
the intellect,

shakes asses.
There's comfort in the mirrorball, slur of
light-flash,
the body's ineloquent thump
                        spun through the crowd.
Let even Wednesday
carry us through, spill us out
and gather us.
Fun,

surprise us, blow smooches,
                              tell me
a good one down here in the dark,

giggle our fool heads off, a few hours
                    gulping the vintage
            of now
      and now and

now

since these moments will have no cellar-life.

Fess Up

I'm early enough to catch
an unsullied sniff
of ocean,
      to pull a lungful.
Seagulls circle a hematite harbour,
their

wings' slim blades
hack
    down from watercolour
cumulus. Row-houses crouch, clapboard-faded,

pressed in a leaning conspiracy
behind the market's stippled sights
of brown cabbage leaves, pop
cans, and trash
        sorted by the bored seasons.

Sixth hour
of day, nightshift finished—left
back there in the dark—
where tables stacked with upturned chairs
point chrome

at a tavern skylight.

Odd jobs, under-
the-table eked-out wages,
days of little turbulence but no
clear route to getting somewhere—I'm returning again
to a friend's borrowed couch
        in a basement on Union,

while the sun's healthy blush
leaks into office towers.

The first
proprietors unlock their metal gates, a
domino clack

cracking the air, tentative, momentary
                              in the grey
a.m. of this neighbourhood. Already

cars cruise near alley-ends

in earshot

of a prostitute who whistles, squints
and waits
with a weariness that seems to say

I was too late for my own life.

Here, for this hour of mine, I understand
how someone could kill
for the contents of a wallet

and not care—

with weeks, then months looking for work,
living south of Main,
                              half of some days
in the welfare-office line-up
to collect a cheque,
                              demoralized
by each implicating glance, feeling useless to
the outer world, and worse,

to any inside project of belonging.

And now, walking home, I pass
a woman
sprawled in the corner of an automatic
teller, blindly trying
to force a needle up
                              into her elbow

and if I add that she's pregnant
though her own life
              has hardly begun,
would you believe in the simple difference
of a few lucky breaks—?

Lucky
your life, lucky my own,
        if something is promised
past that despair:
because of some fortune or circumstance,
of education, or work,

friends, family,

the love that's just given us, and
we didn't even ask.

Winter Walking

Winter. Another
night to go gloved,
more footprints of flattened snow
to fall into.

Trudge.

Icy branches rattle, half-formed in this world.
There's a conditional truce
in the weather, a few
fickle degrees around zero.
So snowflakes fall
like propaganda leaflets
upon which is written
                    Let peace descend.

I'm not the only one
under a grainy newsreel of dark sky and
flurry, this blizzard-scroll
of half-sketched figures
braced against the cold.
Pity the ones with bad luck all their lives.
Loneliness is not from lack of people
or love; it is the steadiness
of having nothing confirmed.

Oh, what
wants to be.

I want, I want, I want
like shovel-scrapes that cut the crisp air.

More scraps of white fall, flit, skim
to the ground—business cards
of every failed venture, the torn-up
programs
of a recital no one came to.

The benches of plush snow;
now the lights burning in rooms.

I would like to take my life gracefully in
hand, like a violin bow.

A Last Walk

Must be getting close to seven, seven-
thirty. April.
              A long
stroll, gone haltingly everywhere,
no duress in the legs' saunter.

Moving away.
                A last
walk through the glass-
fronts of office towers,
each steel vertex cleaving the cloying whorls of rain.
Stroll through

these brief otherworlds, self-
service fluorescents, half-cleared
parking garage,
underpass, traffic island, the concrete
cloverleafs scrolling into suburbia…

Whatever. Back there and up
ahead,
whatever.

The fresh musk of dead worms in the park's
sunk pitch
fill:
         wind that rushes through lunging maples;
      the web-shadow of a bridge-truss;

everything out here
that's held or left alone.

Diner neon,
squirrel-shook hedge, glow
of taxi roof-light crawling up L'Esplanade.
                                  Let
how I loved to be here
not change, though the objects will.

Steady traffic.
A few
craft-stands closing on the corner.
Summer coming on.

Idleness

Heart
held inside here, wait a while—

What do you hear?
(Hardly anything, hardly anything…)

Silence is not tonelessness; listen.
Untie yourself from straight lines
                           and money,
        traffic, grammar.
Drift.

There is another pace of us;
a time to burn
        and a time to cool

and sometimes the cooling
is better.

Each thought be an hourglass,
each whisky tumbler a murky crystal
that predicts you will sleep tonight
                           even
with all your heartbreak.

There is the sky, three daubs of cloud,
a bit of gossip among the leaves.

The long afternoon a bicycle you can sleepily pedal…

So what if you could've done… should've said…
The persons you never were
                           can't hurt you.

Easy now.

Walking Around

—for Dorothy Jeffreys

Each city, since I left
I've been returning to—
curbs, bus shelters, doorframes,
stoops, the descending view

from the top of steep, one-
way streets that reach down to a square
and some avuncular statue, where
the space whips up a breeze

of polluted cirrus, and slides it across
buffed granite and glass,
above the five o'clock surge of mass
transit. All of those

generic or iconic
shapes of brick and steel—
flat-tops, spires, high-rise and three-storey
walk-ups—still

flit past my mind
in its liquid cradle, transporting me
through striped awnings and intersections, vines,
graffiti and clotheslines.

I'm somewhere else now, but I keep
moving through. My head
strolls the street-life, back
in cities briefly visited—

Vancouver, Kwang-ju, Montreal,
Miyazaki, Tunis, Rome—
If any of them ever felt like home
it's because I wandered those places arguably

enough, but I can't really tell, even
in the little time that's winged by
since then,
where I wanted to get to.

And why go anywhere? Just
that we need a pace to adjust
the mind's anxious racing and slow it,
carry it toward some

hint of destination. And so
I just walked, past wrought-
iron fences, off-ramps, bistros,
monuments and grocery stalls,

down traffic-lapped avenues where crowds
rushed, late for a movie below
uneven ledges that glow
in mid-summer like long, sun-burned collarbones.

And because I often walked,
lingering in each city's new, unfamiliar grid
I was compelled to articulate
a restless part of myself, half-hid

and too uncertain to crack open
easily, until somehow, one day, this sudden
uncluttered question
presented itself: *where will I find*

a place I can live and be happy?
And I took that question, like a dog, for a long
walk, looking down into its unspeaking mug,
a stubborn pug

that shadows me again, turning
back, running ahead,
waiting at the crosswalk. A surprise
if I found I was learning

anything in this self-taught frogmarch
to nowhere. I mean, what
are the chances I'll ever bulls-eye that
skittish, civilizations-old

inquiry? But isn't that the reason
why anyone
walks for long hours, to bounce
the terror of not knowing

what their life is about
off the forms that surround them?
I strolled this doubt
through side-streets home,

markets closing, my boots'
iambic shuffle echoing into alleys
and down man-holed drains
near grey stains

of rotting lettuce, the pedestrianesque
figure of someone looking
for something. *Qu'est-ce que
c'est?* Some reverie,

some undimmed thankfulness,
a peerless moment
where nothing's surrogate, just
is, I guess.

(Wanting now to clarify
that I was not alone,
though a few years gasped by
in that apprenticeship

of being apart from you—and me
still learning to love more
and better…) Even happy,
we'll half-imagine

living in another
world, dumbstruck to say
what we would put there—news,
technology and architecture

that doesn't yet exist beyond a sketch,
floorplan or pasteboard maquette.
Like ghostly ads
of extinct brands—chocolate, hats, cigarettes—

on these brick facades, the past
is not far, suggestive
of the future we're at a loss to shape.
We might find our life in any landscape,

but moreso here. Each city a turnstile
of details, questions, private moments
stirred by *a single weathered threshold*
or the touch of a single tile

or today,
this corner and a dampness in the air.
What am I looking for?
Where was I going, anyway?

Notes

The Camus quotes that appear on the title page and as an epigraph to "To the Minotaur" are both taken from the essay "The Minotaur, or The Stop in Oran" which appears in Albert Camus's *The Myth of Sisyphus and Other Essays.*

"Grass"
The translation of four lines of Tu Fu's poem, "Loneliness," is by Kenneth Rexroth (*One Hundred Poems from the Chinese*).

"Photograph of the Funeral Pyre of Pol Pot"
It is believed that over 20 000 men, women, and children were questioned, tortured and put to death at S-21 (Tuol Sleng), the Khmer Rouge's interrogation centre. Factory workers nearby, who could guess what was happening there, described the centre as "the place [where people] went in and never came out."
This photograph appeared on the front page of *The Guardian Weekly*, week ending April 26, 1998.

"The Turofsky Collection"
Pioneers of sports photojournalism, Lou and Nat Turofsky photo-graphed the Original Six hockey teams for almost thirty years, from the 1920s to the 1950s. The Collection is housed at the Hockey Hall of Fame in Toronto.

"Letter to Auden"
Fifth stanza: The italicized lines are taken from Auden's poem "Woods," the second poem of his "Bucolics."
Ninth stanza, lines 8 & 9: see section II of Auden's "In Memory of W.B. Yeats."
Nineteenth stanza, lines 3 & 4: see section I, stanza 26 of Auden's "Letter to Lord Byron."

"Walking Around:"
The italicized lines in stanza 27 are excerpted from a 1929 essay by Walter Benjamin, quoted in Edmund White's *The Flâneur.*

In Acknowledgement

The author would like to acknowledge the generous support of the
Canada Council for the Arts, the Ontario Arts Council and the Banff
Centre for the Arts while writing this collection.

A few of these poems appeared in *Arc, Books in Canada, The Danforth
Review, Descant,* and *The Malahat Review.*

Friends and family are breathlessly acknowledged.
Thank-yous to the good people at the Manx Pub.
For specific comments and good talks regarding these poems, thanks
to: Don Coles, Dennis Lee, Jan Zwicky, Steven Heighton, Tim
Bowling, Suzanne Buffam and Ken.
Don McKay used his loving set of chisels and planes on sundry
excesses; I'm in debt to that honesty and intelligence (Thanks, Don!).

*D*avid O'Meara was born and raised in Pembroke, Ontario. He has lived, for varying periods, in Ottawa, Vancouver, and Montreal, as well as Japan and South Korea, working as a bartender, maintenance worker, and English-language instructor. He is the author of one previous collection of poetry, *Storm still* (1999, McGill-Queen's University Press), shortlisted for the Gerald Lampert Memorial Award. He has been published in a number of literary magazines and recently appeared with Michael Ondaatje in *Where the Words Come From: Canadian Poets in Conversation* (2002, Nightwood Editions).